The Floating World

Seraphim George

First edition, 2025

ISBN (Paperback): 979-8-9998878-4-9
ISBN (Hardcover): 979-8-9998878-5-6

Published by Quo Vadis Press
Boston, MA

Printed in the United States of America

To Elder Savvatey Ageyev,
whose counsel and prayers
lift me high above the floating world.

Introduction

Poems arrive, for me, in moments I am unwilling to lose.
They begin in a sudden jolt of recognition: a bird lifting from
a branch in early light, the shock of surf against my ankles, a
face that stays too long in memory, or the echo of a saint's
voice caught between dream and waking. These are not
extraordinary moments. They belong to the ordinary days,
the passing world. But I have always felt the need to hold
them still, to give them a form that endures. Each poem
begins as an act of keeping, of saying: this is worth not
forgetting.

    The Floating World gathers together over a decade of
such acts. Most of the poems within it were first scattered
across three collections: *Milkweed for Monarchs*, *A Swiftly Tilting
Shore*, and *Dear Seamus Heaney*. Each of those books can easily

stand alone, carrying their own atmosphere and set of concerns. *Milkweed for Monarchs* grew from my fascination with transformation, with the fragile balance of the natural world. *A Swiftly Tilting Shore* circled questions of love, friendship, and faith, written as I found myself shifting between different kinds of relationships and different kinds of devotion. *Dear Seamus Heaney* was a book of homages and dialogues, poems that sought conversation with the dead and with the living who shaped me. I quickly sensed, however, that the boundaries between those books were more porous than I originally imagined. Many of them were written years apart and seemed to speak to one another. I realized that what I thought of as three separate bodies of work were actually fragments of one larger whole, my poetic voice during years of turmoil and growth. And so *The Floating World* was born: an attempt not to erase the earlier collections but to allow them to drift together into one shape, one continuous arc.

The title comes from the Japanese phrase *ukiyo*, which means "the floating world." Originally it referred to the fleeting, transient world of pleasures: the theater, the teahouse, the market streets of Edo. But beneath it lies the Buddhist recognition that all things are impermanent, shifting, without anchor. As an Eastern Orthodox Christian, I face the same concept in our theology: that the world, with all its passions and distractions, is floating away, impermanent. The only thing that matters, that will really last, is our soul. That soul wrote these poems in the midst of all the world floating around me. My poems are born out of delight in the fleeting, but are also shaped by the knowledge of their passing away. To live in a floating world is to live with both beauty and loss, with presence and absence.

The structure of the book reflects this drift. It is divided into five parts, each one circling a particular set of images and concerns, but all meant to be in conversation with one another.

The first section, *Shorelines and Skies*, begins in the natural world. These are poems of weather, of seas and ponds, of dragonflies and rain. They draw from the landscapes that have always compelled me: the New England shoreline, the gray wash of Nantucket, the quiet stir of Acadian waters. To begin here is to begin with the physical world, the world that gives shape to the metaphors of our inner lives.

The second section, *Islands and Journeys*, turns to exile and return. These are poems of distance, of being a stranger, of walking under stars, of dreaming of harbors. They are restless poems, moving between places and people, between the desire to belong and the inevitability of departure. The island, in these poems, becomes both a refuge and a trap: it holds us, and it keeps us apart.

The third section, *Moonlight and Absence*, gathers poems of intimacy and loss. Here love becomes fragile, sometimes fleeting, sometimes enduring only in memory. These are the poems where silence and distance speak as loudly as words. Moonlight, with its cold beauty, seemed to me an emblem of this kind of love: it illuminates even as it reminds us of what is absent.

The fourth section, *Gods and Monsters*, moves into the mythic. Here appear the old stories: Sisyphus, Icarus, Nephilim, prophets and saints. These figures arrive not as distant myths but as presences that haunt our contemporary lives. They live in their own world, not one that is floating away around me but one that floats above, just outside my vision, slightly out of reach. They remind us that we live with the weight of stories older than ourselves, that the old gods are never fully gone, nor the old fears. In these poems, the border between sacred and profane blurs, and myth presses against the modern.

Finally, the fifth section, *Shadows and Fire*, draws the collection to its end. These poems face mortality, inheritance, the reckoning of who we are and what we leave behind. They are poems of philosophy and memory, of fathers and sons, of belief and disbelief. They end at the threshold between the wild and the domestic: the hunter and the hearth, violence and rest, the call of the wild and the claim of home. To close here is to admit that no poem can resolve these opposites, but perhaps poetry can hold them in tension for a moment longer.

Across all five parts runs a single thread: the attempt to listen for what vanishes. Poems, for me, are a way of paying attention to what is slipping away, the shimmer of water, the face of a lover, the voice of a prophet, the long shadow of history. They are ways of saying: I have seen this, I have felt this, and I want it to be known, even if only for the span of a page.

What unites these poems, I think, is not their subjects but their longing. Longing for presence in the midst of absence, for meaning in the midst of loss, for permanence in a world that floats. I realize the answers to the impermanence of the world are found, for me, in Christianity. I also realize this is not where countless others have found their answers; in fact, many still find themselves searching for what really matters, for something greater to serve as an anchor in the currents of a disappearing world. And so, if there is any faith that everyone can relate to in the pages of this book, it is the faith that language, though fragile, can carry us a little way further in trying to make sense of it all, that a poem can keep company with both our joy and grief, and may even steer us closer to the source of that longing.

I do not know if these poems will endure. After all, I'm just one writer among thousands, and, like me, this book will disappear one day, as impermanent as the world in which it was written. Most of what any of us write is forgotten anyway, from the notes and journals of the greatest authors to the unpublished novels of the least-known authors. But I hope that for those who read this book, the poems might linger for a time, might hold close something of your own fleeting days. And if they do, then they will have done what I asked of them when I first set them down on paper.

- Seraphim George, 2025

Table of Contents

I. Shoreline & Skies

Where Dragonflies Commune

I sit under the pine tree,
hidden, observing from a bench
the sanctuary past my house,
down my road, a mile round the bend.

The scene is saturated green,
sun-light dapples dance between trees
swaying over clover, straw, and grass,
where dragonflies commune with bees.

I am lost in the smell of earth,
wood, moss, and fragrant flowered herbs,
lost in winged patterns of swallows,
the sea of reeds the wind disturbs

across an open field. Its waves
of light race across its surface.
Behind it stands a forest wall,
epic in stature. In that place

the mystic, columned hall is formed
with woven roof, and below,
a thousand flowers grow in groups
like white blankets of summer snow.

Here, I forget a mile off
the scent of gasoline,
and metallic, noisy, man-made things
dash solitude to smithereens.

Demeter's Call

It's January still,
but you would not know it,
except for trees which stand
now nude and sunbathing
in an extraordinary
interruption.

Persephone escaped today,
heard Demeter's call
and through the earth rose up,
reached out onto the surface.
She touched it,
just before her husband
pulled her back to Hades.

Sitting in her fingerprint,
the smell of spring unnatural
but welcome.

Like the bogs before me,
stripped and dull, yet having thrown
a remnant to their edge along
the sallow turf, this is
a day incarnadine, not dun,
a post-it note for spring.

Earth Child

Little verdant child,
peering out
from underneath
a peaky, woolen blanket.

The clouds had tucked her in.

She wakes because she hears
the Father's call.
Soon she'll be arrayed
in floriated fashion

and coiffured
with iridescent jewels,
prepared to greet
the saffron sky of spring.

Biography of an Ant

A movement on inverted granite sky
with hair-like legs that escalate behind,
a foot to go, for him a thousand miles.

A one-ton crumb lies upon his shoulders,
fallen from an old man's decrepit hands
giving bread to doves to find his meaning.

Some instinctual beast-call, some duty
to the Mother causes it to stumble.
And to what end? Think of it.
His obstacles are harder to defeat

with that bread crumb. The sun, through glass upheld
by youthful brats, has baked his kind before.
Now it beats on him with birds who hunt,

who watch his way, wait patiently to strike.
The food he carries doesn't help his case.
For pity's sake, it makes them drool the more.
And where is this wayward traveler's home?
The hole is near. He senses it, feels it,
the instinct of another draws him there.

But though he doesn't know exactly where:

like Poles Point or Chatham Light or on the Knob
off Woods Hole Way, his path is marked off well.

I hope he lives. From here I cannot tell.

Harbored Storm

Falmouth Harbor lays before me, tortured,
confused, abused by an arresting unseen wrath,
uncharacteristically whipped up.
Thrown upon the dock, cold and violent

waters weave pandemonic wave with wave
and form an agitated, anxious spread
of foam and rippled bedlam, thrown over
the abysmal secrets of the sea.

An air-brushed expansion of foam, unrolled
from me to the Elizabethan Islands,
writhes in the likeness of the sea below.
The smooth, slate and undulating mass

of unshed storm, despairing its burden,
vehemently seeks to let it go,
rolls onward vexed and frustrated,
to the place where it can be released again.

I sit between the dismal sea and sky,
tossed by the same impassioned winds that blew
the clouds and surf, bewailing me to tears,
and like the setting, splitting me in two.

The Floating World

I am alone, like a willow tree
cut off at the root. I want to float
where the water flows to take me.

Clouds sail on a sea of constant blue
while day after day the sun rises,
then falls to the onslaught of the moon.

Like them I just go on, drifting,
drifting like the colored maple leaves
floating down the frosted wood-streams

of Bourne Farm and yellow fields of straw
adrift upon the autumn breeze,
before the coming of a bitter snow.

Fish Monger

The walls are dark-stained wood, the bar the same,
asking my imagination to recall
the days of fishermen and whale men,
and now those men of old have lost their claim

to oceanographers and sun-burned tourists.
Heavy smells linger here, of fresh-caught fish,
burgers, French fries in the fry-o-later,
which spatter grease and toss a savory mist

into the atmosphere. Conversation,
heckled with the interrupting clang
of silverware and plates, orchestrates a hum.
In front of me, a screen quilts a pattern

on the windowed scenery, letting in
the salty, seaweed air. Just outside,
water blankets up against the weathered docks,
bathes the land and salted population.

This place is a clever disinfectant,
cleansing zombish minds, like mine, of stress.
My sandwich comes. The waitress gives a smile,
mumbles something nice and turns, tip-expectant.

Of Wakeby Pond

He's dead, underneath the agued coffin-Ld,
The static, blackened vault of Wakeby Pcnd.
I heard through friends his dog deceived him once,
Seducing him onto the ice at dawn.

Winter played her part, reassuring him
The blanket, spun with winter's thread of frost,
Was safe. He trusted that maleficence,
Who hides in peaceful white, a blackened rot.

Now the spring has rules which haven't changed.
The beauty here: the birds, the trees, the brisk air
Disguise the morbid truth of what occurred,
His bloated, banished body lying still, out there.

The waves of saw-grass chill when thinking how
He feeds them now, invigorates their growth.
Dancing on their captive, mocking that they've won,
They drown him once again in muck-draped root.

But wait - Perhaps his sleep is not so bad
On pebbled bed, with rush's rooted spread.
And when he wakes he'll see the mingled sun,
Distorted sky, and shadowed feet of swans.

'Sconset

Melancholic cottages in droves
scramble for the sea in layer
tumbling over layer,
splash on stilts upon the breakers.
They flatter the sea, a mimicry
of shingle over weathered shingle,
gray as the Nantucket dawn,
riddled with cracks and dents and grooves:
products of wind and time
like a battered wave's surface.

Time passes. Observations fly.

No more distinct, the masses
fall united with the deep,
each cottage a wave,
each street a current,
each rotary a whirlpool,
around which white-capped houses swirl,
each block a gale,
the village a tempest.

I walk between the crests
with friends, with villagers,

with other traveling guests,

who float upon the sea:

the sea at 'Sconset.

On Six Foot Wings

I am surrounded by celestial beauty,
overwhelmed by mountainous expanse,
the vulture's dance
on six foot wings upon the snowy wind.

I have met Elijah's ravens
souring up to cavernous nests
of sticks and tamarack,
as if they come to feed me
on the mountain's barren peak,
black angels of God,
messengers from a holy realm
to keep their eye on one
alone.

Rain

Hear the rain as it falls to soothe the soul
By sound and music, a saturating choir
Of wet and shifting light. Old river's refuse,

Having once fallen, rises, ascends upward,
Glorified and waiting for its coming
Twice again, and after, parachuting down

To rest in tingling ears and bladed grass,
Filling gutters round the roof, and rushing proof
That rivers run again. Can you remember

entering its sun-soaked after glow,
Marveling the subtle pearls and wet jeweled plants,
A ragged dance of prisms, lost in new sun's light?

Rainbows live there, in Noahic after-light,
Like covenant's peace, still and meditative,
Come as promise after forty days and nights.

And that same rain rung in the patriarch's ear,
Heard by millions a hundred thousand times, then
Heard by you. Perhaps tonight it comes again.

Acadian Waves

Waves shepherd me

into your kingdom,

empire of mist, light

and holy places,

saturating souls

and bringing dew

to arid spaces,

until I'm overcome,

sprouting tears like shoots

from weather-beaten rock.

The Sea By Tennyson

What sea, that dances on the furrowed moor,
Could quell my sorrows, quench my fears as this,
When, stretching out from me, only to kiss
The mouth of some as yet unchartered shore?

My mind does wander from this precipice,
Beneath this ocean, playground to the free,
Where mysteries and beasts of darkness be,
Rising from the fearful, blackened-blue abyss.

And now I sit to watch the setting sun,
Where sea and sky and light become enmeshed,
My spirit, knowing it will be refreshed,
The world's woes a little more undone.

Surf

Thunder has been done to death.

Rather, it is the response
of arrogance to war:
an applause that drowns
the cannons
of war,
both sounds mingling
in violent approbation.

Sizzling
pan bacon
seething, searing
in its grease.
Leaves whoosh
in a thousand
forest shades,
countless ruined
poems tossed
away.

The waves
leave water-veins
within a golem's

tawny skin,

trickling

down,

inhaled

by the

swell,

until the thunder comes again.

And at the crash, the water billows up,

a white cumulonimbus

racing over golden plains of rock and wheat.

Behind the cloud,

an aquatic sky

of liquid jade:

a peace,

translucent

in the sun.

The milk from water,

a first miracle

more tame,

more subtle

at the place

of fumbling froth

and ochre rocks,

spread thin,

like cobwebs

swept across

the mirror's glass.

Description of the Sea from a Boat

The very color blue is shaken,
fractured into countless shades,
tumbles, crashes, and disperses
one within the other, symbols
of divine magnificence, a sacred
revelry of light and wet and sky,
every body panting to delight.

In God's making, unseen hands
knead the water's swell, a dough
that, when mixed with sun and surface-play
will turn to awe and bliss and praise.

And there's no land. There hasn't been
for days, yet how is it that I feel
grounded, like the seagulls scattered
on the wind, kites that hover
in their hundreds, ride the seaweed smell
of brine and sickly rotting fish
and salted air, yet feel secure there,
as if they stood on solid ground.

Windows

Outside the windows fly
of another world, another life,
window to window passing
like strangers, like light wintry airs,
inconsequential, unrestrained.

And trees, buildings, people,
the harbor tweaked with moon
and pale lamps, fraternal twins
that dance upon the waves and time,
pass like film along the glass,
along the cool rigid touch
of a translucent gaze
into a transient companion
of a world, until it disappears.

All of it: all this dies,
is buried at my back
under the soil of my periphery
never to be raised. And if I turn
it is altogether something different:
changed and running away.
I think of death,
of passing lives and trees
and windows.

A Mirrored Image

Like a school boy's whistle
at a passing girl, the bird sings.
Crayon-yellow breasted feathers,
bright orange beak, folded black wings
mold the bird. It repeats its cry.
Within, it calls to me.

The brush bounces, moving suddenly
above the tiny tree-topped glass.
A sacrificial sight appears:
a moth flaps desperate in the grass.
The bird falls quickly on its prey.
There is a breeze today

ruffling my clothes as I watch,
disheveling the finch's feathers too,
as it enjoys its catch alone.
Back to the water's edge it dips
its head, spoons the water lightly
lifting up to wash it down,

repeating silence once again,
making sure the bitter taste of bug

and fleshy crumb consumed.

Then it stills, looks at me, flies away.

I'll leave as well, a woebegone

disconsolate to wander.

II. Islands & Journeys

Stranger in this Land

The truth: it is who I am,
a stranger in an old, forsaken land.
On our ship, my captain steers and I,
through wind tossed seas just stand

and wonder how this blemished,
lifeless land was once a golden shore.
A stark disquiet issues from my heart,
for I've been here before

and remember once not long ago
I also lived on this unhallowed ground,
but left upon this vessel found,
whose captain had unbound

my heart, immersing in despair,
and caused my blinded eyes to plainly see,
I'm a stranger in this land: who I am,
who I was meant to be.

Pointers

Jump left. Turn right. Now run
along the russet shore
where wood meets gilded fields.

Their masters run behind,
blowing into wind the whistle calls.

They follow
spotting birds
escaping
into aromatic sunset smells
of earth tone tamarack.
They run, ears flopping,
palpable excitement
galloping like horses.
They stop. They point.
Good dog.
They wag their tales
and run through endless
sunburst possibilities.

They are confined by rules,
calls, commands,
but I envy them.

They are free,
bound in chains
among their masters.

I long to run and catch birds,

to be free.

Like Humankind

In a tense and violent storm
the great tree fell. I saw it,
lying in his throes.

I thought then of the cycles
during which he stood, patient there
in his appointed place.

A thousand times or more, the tree
beheld the earth and burst to bloom,
amid the happy songs

of mating birds. A thousand summers
beautified his flesh with a crystal
crown of jewels,

beaming in a shifting storm's sun.
And every night for all those years
he stood alone

upon that hill, rogue and silent
in the lonely light of a white
and mystic moon.

Waking from a Dream

When I leave the island, without fail,
I feel as if I'm waking from a dream,
stuck upon a vessel somewhere sailing
in the moon and morning.

I see the dream, a distant sunset haze
exhausting form and breadth and color,
captured in between an Eden lost
and Purgatory gained,

bound to lost ideals of peace, nostalgia,
longing and fulfillment, faith in God,
who conjures light from utter darkness
smoldering in the void.

When I leave the island, without fail,
I feel as if I'm waking from a dream.

Walking under Stars on Nantucket

Walking under stars on Nantucket
I am a lone lighthouse weaving beams
with night air, beckoning to ships and angels.
In the utter darkness I'm unafraid
of creatures roaring from the sea,
of angry dunes cast by shadows
with my flashlight, furrowing their brows
as light moves across the sand, meets shadow,
and they disappear.

Unmoved by my blind periphery,
I'm guided rather by the smell of brine,
the sound of depth.
Here, I see with my heart and come to rest
on mist-wet sand that clumps between my toes,
cool and unchained.

But even now, through the darkness,
clarity begins to seep
into the understanding of a night.
The stars begin to cast their ancient light
and the surf explodes upon my vision
in froth and violence and ghostly apparitions
that coalesce and then recede.

Nantucket

I

Nantucket: island of my heart, within
its rhythmic soundings lost to the pulsing
of the sea's perimeter, throwing up
its sand upon the waves, as a white flag
in the calm anticipation of peace.

Placed within a body of dark terrors
and beasts of unfathomable power,
where storms dance over a lachrymose floor
in intemperate worship, uncaring,
unanswerable to anyone but God.

II

People school like fish
upon its shores
in search of food
strewn across the cobblestone,
of shelter, of friendship.
Every year they swim
on surface sands,
inelegant

yet lithe, a sign of safe
discomfort, a turbid light.
Like clouds they come
to carry off the sun,
dissipating
on the ferry home.

III

The Lady Grey
vanishes from sight,
with a glimmer,
a wink and a nod,
in the exhale
of a dying sun.

The Grey Lady

Do I sail away from her,
or does she sail away from me?

Subsumed in fog, she floats
upon a still, sleet ocean,
vanishing within a swath
of mist and magic,
the ghost of a dream,
not terrible or lost
but melancholy.

She's like a lover's body
lost to endless fathoms,
beautiful and still,
becoming less distinct
and sinking down,
down into the depths
beneath the surface gray.
A final strip of sand
that glows like amber through the mist
is like a final strand
of golden hair that waves
within the current,
lashes out until it disappears.

She sails away from me,
lover to a desperate heart
with all my joys
and expectations anchored there,
like when a lover
turns to walk away
on a day of rain and grief,
robbing me of dreams.
I stare into the fog,
imagining that she's still there,
another beach or even just a light,
wanting desperately to catch
a final glimpse of where I was.

But sea meets sky uninterrupted,
their frontier edges blurred,
and once again I drift
upon unending waves.

Ship of Sand

Sailing on a ship of sand,
breaking through the waves
with the bow at 'Sconset
and standing on its tip,
I am captain
of this Nantucket ship,
my own destiny's maker:

explorer, fisherman, whaler.

But inevitably,
I'll face opposite the wind
and let it push me
towards civilization,
the realization
that I'm simply just a man
on a beach, after all.

Metamorphosis

Today I watched a hapless swallowtail,
intermingled black and yellow movements
vivified with summer skill, set sail

until, with barbarous and ambushed sweep,
a tanager dove down and pulled it up
in frank aggression, and, as if to keep

the moment begging for its poignant end,
released its prey which panted up, spun round,
collapsed and struggled for its flight again.

Struck, carried for a bit, and then released,
a morbid dance performed before my eyes,
a vaulting dissonance of motion ceased

when reverberant designs, now blanched,
grew impotent and lost, imprisoned by
the crushing talons poised upon the branch,

kaleidoscopic wings pressed down and bruised,
perverse and twisted up behind itself,
a beauty ravishing and rent, subdued

by captor, muscular and virulent.
Down, up, thrust down again, the stout beak worked.
Wing-dust glittered like the faerie's remnant

innocence when startled into thin air,
as above, the tree leaves bounced and trembled
in the strain of violated nature.

Assaulted, butchered, leg by leg dismembered,
one by one plucked off to make digestion
smoother, a flying jewel sad-remembered

in the twilight of another day,
now gone, its two wings floated, lingered on,
beginning their descent into decay.

Sandy Meditation

As I was praying on my sanded shrine,
A hipped girl walked by; a tall, fine specimen,
Who made me wonder if I'll always be
Indebted with the ample price I have to pay
For ruttish sins until I turn to dust,
Or if I'll turn from monkery, to love again

Spanish Amah

She cleans with quiet fortitude,
humbly scraping off their fecule grease
with chipped and work-worn nails.
Beneath the garden's orange tree, a line
runs another's clothing, the sun-dried soul
of who she wants to be. From the kitchen
comes heavy grime-sizzled smells of thieving
cookery, mixing sweat and oil and spice.

She knows that Terra-cotta roofs,
that marble floors and roman porches
lording over glowing pools,
imported gold-leaf, lapis lazuli,
and oak-arched doorways to a Spanish villa
cannot hide interior designs.

She wanders, washing dishes
by the window, looking out
onto the Roman pillared patio,
listens to the birds, the winds
of Africa that rustle palm trees
big enough to build a house for her.
She listens to the rush of cars
and motorbikes, of life without,

anything to keep away
her ears and eyes from life within.

She barely hears the child's cries of pain,
begging to relent, each slap for them,
a slap for her as well. Tears, released
but useless, are wiped away as screams
crescendo into helplessness
and all she does is wipe away the blood.

In the silent night, when all her work is done
and the moonlight's quiet serenade falls
on tired ears, she mules to quarters
of her own, behind the big house. As she leaves,
the night's silence isn't sound enough
to cover up a mother's crying
soft inside, pouring still another drink.

She shuts the iron door, masks the misery,
trying to efface it from her memory.

Tomorrow she'll be forced to see once more.

Terra Firma

I'm trying to engrave in mind
terra firma left behind
to the African Sun,
baked into brick and soaked in oil.

Ground rises up, reaches
around rivers, rolling on,
lifting rows of olive groves
along the highway,

Panoramically spread out
over a sanguine earth.
The Mediterranean
fringes my periphery,

mingling surf with dark-red dust
in lapis lazul blue.
Along the coast, scattered
over mountain slopes, the cities lie

in Spanish grandeur: villas
floored and pillared marble,
robed in bleach-white stucco,
crowned with terra-cotta terraces,

which gaze for miles

out to hollow distances,

from where I strain to see below,

resign myself to say goodbye.

The Cucking Stool

Affliction is the cucking stool of life.
We ensconce ourselves within its torrent,
respire its polluted water, to drown:
a sure end.

I live deformed, unable to sustain
the weight of tribulation, am trampled
by the aching ever-presence, the sin
of ennui,

deceived, saronged by the world's venal yoke.
But my voice remains unburdened, immune
from the resistance of acedia,
so I cry,

wail to the sea and to its god, who hears,
breaking from the depths of my ordeal,
erupting from its adamantine face,
to echo.

1945

A day full of mist, clouds and slow rain.
Two people standing, doomed,
two strangers, trembling, scared, confused.
They've been released from life, just stare
into a void of shock and hopeless grief,
imagining their isolation,
ineffably reserved.

Giving up was not an option; living was,
but they'll succumb, eventually.
They'll die a sacrifice.

You marched until the sun went down;
withered, creased, dolorous,
knowing nothing can undo the pain
that's sweeter still than that which was to come.
Along the road, your languid people move,
slow, pondering your isolation,
ineffably reserved.

Giving up was not an option; living was,
but you'll succumb, eventually.
You'll die a sacrifice.

Seven hundred miles from home, unknown,
and lit by peaceful moonlight.
In front of us, a guard, a banner,
stars that shimmer, out of darkness breaking,
but around us, shadow, rotting mounds,
the place bereft, isolated,
ineffably reserved.

Giving up was not an option; living was,
but we'll succumb, eventually.
We'll die, a sacrifice.

I watch and wait. I hope not yet, not yet
and turn to view the camp.
Infested clouds of bloated flies follow
bodies heaped in a memory of goodness.
I hear my name. A tear as still I stand,
resigned to isolation,
ineffably reserved.

Giving up was not an option; living was,
but I'll succumb, eventually.
I'll die, a sacrifice.

A day full of mist, clouds and slow rain.
Where do they stand, the doomed,

the strangers, trembling, scared, confused?
They've been released from death, just spared,
freed from shock and the weight of hopeless grief,
an escape from isolation,
ineffably reserved.

A Door Into the Dark

All I know is a door into the dark,"
one poet said. So let my door disclose
to readers what I see, to take them
to my spirit's home, the weathered hallmark
showing how I live, think, grieve, compose.

I often wonder if my conjugated
thoughts, ideas and illustrations fit
for what emotion the occasion warrants,
if all too often my dramatic moments
generate a gloomy state, instigate
like mud which, with its slurping, gurgling,
gobbledygook array of suction sounds,
sticks to the passerby and brings him down.

A Letter and a Toast

Last night I sat and took in more than whiskey.
I took another's sorrow, made it mine.
Black shirt, blue jeans, perfectly matched
and by the end even to the inner man.

Please, I plead with you, don't take from me
your comfort's ease, like others have.
Don't turn away before I get to say
I care, I'll be there when the others fade.

You see, I've written words like these before,
only to erase their arbitrary name,
and while nothing's guaranteed, we'll fight
to free ourselves from fears of being tossed aside.

Last night, though at times subdued by carking gloom,
we discovered joviality again,
with singing, clapping, laughing, soon forgetting
life lay waiting to remind us

after Liam's pub and song, that waking up
will wallow us in teared realities.

My constant friend, whatever shadows come

remember Liam's, that good still exists,

and lithe enthusiasms, promises

of better days and simpler, steady breath.

A Swiftly Tilting Shore

He stares across the room
at empty walls. He listens,
waits. He cannot hear her breathe.
He doesn't move,

just stares ahead and listens,
listens, listens, knowing how
she's gone to the black sea
on waves of release,

her color evanesced
to canvas, washed out
and something else changed:
she remained, hollowed.

Now he falls into the sea
from a swiftly tilting shore,
borrowing her fate
to sink, to drown, to feel

into the depth-shrouds
of forgetfulness,
too tired to swim
or build a raft and oar.

III. Moonlight & Absence

An Act of Marriage

Sear it forever in my mind,
and let it radiate from there,
a sun to warm
my ice soul-nights.

Persevering to remember
this guignol act, played out for me,
two wood-beams merged,
forever joined

in the Golgotha of my mind,
the fell, on which you died instead:
two beams, never
to be divorced.

Let me hear throughout the ages
that ceremony's wedding bells.
Let them free me
with their ringing.

A Riparian Drama

Hermaphroditus and the nymph
exchange their glances,
passing by like lovers
impassioned by the fervid sun.

She drags her blue and milky hand
across his talus skin,
stroking, turning his face
though still but not unmoved, entranced

by the pounding of her steps,
the ripples of her dress
that fruitlessly obscure
her body's taut, quivering contours.

He draws her in until they kiss
upon a bed of sand
and pulse and roll and move
upon and in each other, one.

An Admiration

If you turn your face,

I'll admire your feet,

feet smudged by pavement and rain,

ankles sore from subway stairs,

your body balanced

on blistered arches.

Sacred wanderer,

I know your face.

Your eyes, lit like storefront glass,

spill their honey

into the night air,

sweet against the grit.

But I admire your feet.

I love your feet

because they carried you

through laundromats and bus stations,

over bridges rinsed in headlights,

through broken glass and summer weeds,

until they found me.

Borrowed Time

The walls are tarnished to a sallow pall.
On them, dust-filled shelves, haphazard pictures,
plaques and bulletins float sporadically
upon their surface, like oily meat chunks
in a moldy stew of soul-indigestion.
Do I want to live in this and simmer?
It breeds coagulating abdication,
a life you swallow just to get it down
to where it sits, heavy.

The air is heavy too,
like grandma's bedclothes in a sealed attic,
festering in mildew and borrowed time.

Clocks

Without purpose,
breath is just a clock

ticking,
ticking,
ticking.

I long to leave this school,
a postcard sent and soon
will just be sitting stagnant,
buried with the others.

They too will disappear.

The earth has taken heavy breath again,
so say the bells. They used to resonate
their witness then that God breaths life
and we inhale His exhale.
Now it's been forgotten.

One such ticking clock once said,
We're here to serve, not to be served,
and He has long since stopped, or so is said.
His gears have ground to dust.

The problem is they preach the clock,
ignore the hopeless consequence
of their Darwinian philosophy.
If, for just one interrupted moment,
we could glimpse the coming day when all will cease
and sand no longer falls, then those who teach,
and if not teach, then live, the lie
(that meaning now and meaning's god are dead,
that crime is just a natural thing we try
along with those we love, worth little more
than dirt, and who's to judge what's true?)
would rather change their trite convictions

than admit the longing of their souls,
awakened at the edge of pardon
and the terror of life's sunset dawning,

can never be attained.

Coffee Shop

I shimmer through a slick and sullen
winter rain, into an orange glow,
to bathe and brew in aromatic mist.

Crowding in on either side are voices
laughing, chatting, forgetting outside
the gray sun stiffens bone to marrow.

Dreams become our day: a tired man's guest,
each cup we drink, a weight from off our chest,
and Carpe Diem coursing through our veins.

I've been coming here almost every day
to find Calliope, who sips her tea,
a brew of skill, of drive, and destiny.

Don't Tell Me that I'm Young

I'm young.

As if I cannot feel the airborne sting
of a million locust thoughts.
They pester me, a young choice grain
that stands in solitude.

I'm young.

As if the weight of tired years at twenty six
is feather-lite, not weighty as the night.

I'm young.

As if a man, bloated and distorted,
drowned in his own tears
at twenty six feet deep
is less drowned than one at forty.

That's why I wait for you, my love,
at twenty six years young.
If you are God, then come.
If Eve, then I will wait until I wake.

Are you young, too?

Then come and pick these grains
with gleaning hands
before the coming of the years.

Don't tell me that I'm young.

Dreaming Harlequin

Awake I am
the dreaming harlequin,
and nightmares face
my wan reflection,
wandering
their evanescent
shadows.

Asleep I live
in glad forgetfulness
and wake to keep
in quiet solitude,
escaping
the image of a man
to be one.

Driving

Headlights battle the indifferent night,
while here, I'm lost in thought, in deed, in sight.

Outside my window, shadows fly behind
and catch my stare. I turn my head and mind
to he who drives, and all looks fine.

All did, back when the strain upon the air
first throttled me with thick philosophy,
amplified the melancholy drone
of my friend, driving.

What? Could this, our night, be ruined by unwelcome
thoughts?
            Yes, and trampled, spit upon, and bent
to be removed, along with joy and gratitude,
replaced, outdone in bluest griefly hue
of wounds lanced and pouring out forgotten woes.

My God, the guy could act like all was well.
But I know better still.

Silence cannot bully me aside. This way
I'll play along and gaze at widening road,

at flying shadow and indifferent night,

bidding quietude to dry the tear,

caught with my eye's corner, on his hand and wiped away.

Two men together on a lonely road,

one heart breaking, another understanding,

the broken man driving.

We've stopped.

You're home and it's goodbye, I guess.

I'd stay and talk, even though there's nothing

I can do. My door slams, and his does too.

I could give a hug, not like a woman's,

Conceded, but love still needed.

Headlights battle the indifferent night,

while here, I'm lost in thought.

My turn to drive.

Evermore By Day

The night, a cloak of finest threads of shade
Against this beacon fights, which I believe
Is weak. The moon of self-will, which does achieve
A month, is inconstant as light's masquerade.

O moon, I've lost your light which once did aid
This traveler who, upon a winter's eve
Fell into the shadow, which you did weave
Along the way, and despaired when light did fade.

So I will travel ever more by day,
Who's light is strong, not mixed with darkened night,
And shining longer makes the road a quicker way,
So I can rest when fades the greater light,
And turning from the moon of self I may
Receive the sun of truth and with it sight.

Falling Asleep in a Paris Airport

It's been a night of trepidation
across an unlocked breach of sky,
turbulence that caused my jaws to knock,
my mind to ask a hundred times,
how many tons can float in air?

It must be blasphemy, causing men
to reach much closer to their maker,
as if their faith in man has aided
frequent fliers from the Middle Ages
and not for barely thirty years now.

My sandstone eyes begin to close.
Sweaty dankness clings to clothing.
Shoes sink deeper into my fatigue,
every leaden step towards home
a hopeful reason for another.

I sit, under disapproving glares
Of Frenchmen, Monty Python-esque,
abounding ethnic stereotypes,
unfathomable world linguists
in a rush of conversation drone,

dashing to prospective terminals.
They are clashing territories
with tongues no longer crying war
but 'Escuzi moi' and 'Come stai',
hellos and helps and 'Donde es... ?'

It's a veritable smörgåsbord,
a culture delicatessen
I try to paint in full mosaic,
losing words and capability
as heavy eyes sink down defeated.

Home Run

Cut and formed into an able metal stick
Held tightly by its tapering neck,
Rotating slowly, gunning the ball
Of leather, nervous, but professionally

Poised. The crack came, sharp as a gunshot.
A moment of surprised contact stuck,
Then I burst forward to run the course
Around the diamond, past players in shock.

I have to look around in disbelief.
The bystanders jubilantly stand to cheer.
Caught up into the crowd, I nonchalantly
Clasp expectant hands, holding back a tear.

Loss

Sitting on my deck
I look around,
hear the sound
of birds,
intermingled
with the ocean-like
surf song
of stately Oak
and Maple,
shuffling
their branches.

I close my eyes
and realize
that all around
is no relief
from unsustained
and hollow grief.

The neighbor's blinds
are down. Within,
my mother sings.
The trees are blind,
the birds dumb,

the wind deaf
as it carries off
my prayers, draws them
from my breath
to unseen,
unknown ears.

At least alone
this truth is sure:
sun, shade, wind,
bird and butterfly
can't stab you
in the back or lie.

They don't save face.

Loved and Lost

I

Whoever said,
'Tis better to have loved and lost,
than never to have loved at all'?

Liar. You have never loved.

Or loved and never lost,
rested in her cantrip arms,
lighthouse to the lost lover's ship.
They beckoned you like rays of light,
puncturing your soul like knives
through the emptiness of night.
But you rested on their edges,
steel-cold to the vagabond's touch,
soothing to love's fire cracking
in the embers of your heart,
and then you wrote those lies.

But I have lost.

I don't believe your poetry,
your fanciful imagination.

I have lost.

II

Love is, for me, a threadless needle,
a coat with none to wear it
though the world is frigid,
a sea, its waves tumultuous,
symphonic, swirling up, around
like a conductor's wand
yet heard by none,
received by nothing:
there is no sand, no splash, no ears.

A tree falls in a forest,
a man falls for a woman,
but if there are none to hear it
has he ever loved at all?

Yes. Oh yes, and how he loved.

But better if he hadn't.

New Year's Eve

Night dawns another new year
and eve the end of one,
the light undone
with failure in its wake.

Moon-beams haunt my window pane,
breathe the frost, casting halos
through New England air.
In another year, will I sit

to write another poem
of another New Year's Eve,
having phoenixed
through the ashes of a lost cause?

Newspaper Clippings

In a hotel of the Quartier Latin,
built amidst the cozy Paris residents,
a lovesick student, clinging to her dress of satin,
blew his brains out, locked within a certain room,
which later held a legal student
who, after failing his examinations,
      likewise sealed his doom.
The landlord, in a superstitious dread,
declared that none should sleep within the room again,
making it a tomb for furniture instead.
Within a week, a waiter there, accused of theft,
went to that tomb and bled himself to death.

      In fear the owner sold his property
      to a druggist with a greedy, skeptic mind,
      who heard the story with dismissive apathy.
      His wife, a savvy woman, left the room behind
      to spend her nights asleep within the bedroom
      farthest from it, 'till, of course, the man discovered
      this, her newest place of sleep, would be his doom:
      his wife had picked a servants bed to dwell within
      and chose to do her hiding undercover.
      So he swallowed all his pride and poison
      in a fit of jealousy and rage,

and made his way into the room he never feared
in life to die, expiring upon its floor.
His wife, on finding he had exited the stage,
assumed a knife to pierce her heart with grief
and fell upon her husband's hollow, cold relief.

With this suicide, the town pronounced it hexed,
demanding that its door be boarded shut,
but the newest owner kept the neighbors vexed
by laughing at their superstitious rut.
Yet the angry crowds were soon appeased,
for announcements of another building came
and the cursed hotel's destruction that would ease
the swift construction of the Faubourg St. Germain.
The owner, with his Paris bankers met,
to demand a quarter million from the banks,
which only gave him ninety thousand francs,
a sum unable to indemnify his debt.
Too sick to think, too proud to kneel and pray,
he wandered aimlessly to look upon that place
before its quietus the following day,
ascended stairways to the room exempt from grace.

And when the workmen came for demolition,
the fatal chamber, faithful to tradition,
held the man suspended by its beams:

one last hurrah, one final moment's dread,

reliquary of its dark and broken dreams,

    a room to house the dead.

Out In The Rain

Through gray sheen, headlights pierce the water wall,
splashing puddles, dismal monotony,
a line of never-ending cars. Streetlights
shine with the grandeur of the First Coming
on a black and holy night. Even trees,
petitioning for sun, spread forked fingers
to the sky, a cry for rescue from their bland
existence, stripped from countryside except
cement, now stripped of leaves, cold, naked, wet.

Across the traffic-soaked intersection,
lined in compartmentalized, stained stone,
stores sit, a train in atrophy. All are closed
but one. A man talks in The Flower Patch,
caressed by flowered plants and walls, veiled
in oblivion to what's without.
He doesn't see me hidden by the dark
outside his window pane, but I see him,
as the world washes away.

Perhaps the trees
have noticed what those flowers, in the comfort
of their store, have missed, that life comes down to this.

On his phone, the man is yelling now,

a business deal gone wrong or love affair

gone to misery I'm sure, but the outside,

it seems, has found him after all. Disgruntled,

he hangs up, turns off the lights, enveloping

the flowers in a heavy gray, and walks,

head down, into the unrelenting rain.

The Only Thing Between Us

I

The run down joint barely stood out
on Main Street, among shops
and fancier places to eat
with less food for more money.

But we went, and what we lacked
in glitz, we gained in time well spent.
He played it straight, hard-assed, macho
as always, from his speech, his drinks,

all of his remembered days
of school-yard fights and lots of girls,
military drills and war,
every muscled push through life

another score on the board
of manhood. He wished I had more points.
He wished more often I had tossed
the coins of risk. He has some left.

II

I had to laugh a little
at all his complications,
imagining inside
are implications

flying high within his mind,
of me, a faithful kowtow boy,
never falling from the nest,
obdurate as stone,

and there he is, alone
on see-saws, swings, and Ferris wheels,
the dance floor, the bathroom floor,
intelligent enough

to deal with all the issues
spinning round his head,
glimpsed like blurring faces
from a merry-go-round.

Despite the news, luminous,
pressing to denude itself,
I will remain a child,
sparing him the anguish

of broken ice, and hearing

all about the wonder years
I've had to live without,
so I just sit and smile.

III

I noticed your graying hair,
your silent film gestured
quasi- paternal face,
know-it-all eyes,

your hard nose, sharp lips spewing
patriarchy wisdom,
a fortune cookie
once resented.

This time, as we retreat
into the Cape Cod night
and down the crowded street,
I walk beside you.

I'm right where you are,
confident the only thing
that stands between us now
is your goodbye.

Divorce

She is the misery suffered by the widow
who has lived to see her husband's body
cresting on a mound of earth and wood, carried
to eternal halls upon the pyre.
She begins to wail and moan for he who left her
lonely in his wake, watching ravens gloat
and circle, waiting for the fire's remnant.
The wisdom of the sage and prophet strikes
a hollow chord that can't engulf the roar
of all her treasures in the flame and still
she smells the burning flesh of dying dreams.
Before the pyre of her abandoned love,
she sings her grief. With hair bound up, unburdening
her fear, a wild litany of nightmare
and lament: her house invaded, enemies
upon the mere, cadavers at her feet,
slavery, abasement and abuse
until the heavens swallow up his form in smoke.

Morning after morning, she wakes to find him
gone, her bed is empty, waiting for fulfillment
now that he has entered death's dominion,
forever severing their marriage bond.
She wanders in the hollowness of home,
gazing sorrowfully at his vacant desk,

the dining room bereft of all delight,
the windswept yard, the muted ticking clock,
the couches buried underground; what was,
is now no more. Abandoned to her longing,
she lies on his side of the bed and weeps
her elegy of *sorrow, sorrow, all is lost.*
The truth, the future, everything bears down too large,
too silent, too remote, this house, these fields.

If I Just

If I just.
If I just.
If I just.

If I just stopped saying it,
stopped believing that I must
relive a thousand more regrets
when I just don't.

If I just realized my novel,
coming to a store near you,
got out of debt,
skipped it like a slim rock
across a lake of burdens
on the other side,
or found another job,
one that frees me
from the brink
of insanity in drudgery,
or sold poems
like raindrops sold to flowers,
paying the exposure's cost
to grow,
or melted into puddles,
melted into ponds,

melded into lakes,
into rivers, into oceans
of art and purpose.

If I just.

If I just trusted
in a father who knows what's best,
untested and untried,
maybe then I'd stop staying

If I could, I would

just stop.

Then if I just stopped,
relished in, enjoyed
the breath of God shot
down into my bones,
making cells of stone,
a human moving,
renegade through time,
rather than a statue
enslaved to a moment
in the past, chiseled
by resentment,

head turned as if to say,
if I just went that way.

I could be a hundred visions
projected by a hundred other choices
never taken, reflecting just as many
faces of the man I could have been,

but I'm not,
and I can't,
and I didn't.

But there is one thing I must
say, if I just
throw myself before the feet of God.

If I just, then...

A Love Poem

They say that we are not the same,
that your life and mine will be lost,
that I am nothing, and you are everything,
that two such different persons cannot love.
But I will not forget I loved you once,
that you will love me still,
and I still long to die within your arms.

I cannot comprehend their judgments,
their cold philosophies, rendered meaningless,
undone by first love's light.

Together we should confiscate the present
from our enemies, escape to dwell
where none can judge,
where none can say it isn't true,
where milk cascades from skeletal goats
and honey from the rock.

We must flee, exiled from the world,
to where there is no law,
only love.

My Father's Son

I'm my father's son,
and he, his son's father.
Could the logic be any simpler,
the equation any more manifest?
Yet I cannot grasp it
with my mind. Cannot
plumb the depths
of its significance.

IV. Gods & Monsters

Liturgy

The roads are paved with dirt
instead of asphalt gold,
crushed and man-made rock.

The stones are untouched,
unformed into buildings,
those obtrusive dead things.

The tors stand brazen
with brio and buck,
yet unashamed to weep

their rivulet streams
or bleed the red clay
or revel in chartreuse,

and with a thousand trees
worship, casting them out,
a thousand liturgies.

Milkweed for Monarchs

I have seen the milkweed rise from roadsides
in July, rough as the back of hands
that know more work than rest.
Bitter runs the sap,
it oozes vile warning.
But still, the monarchs eat.
Soft mouths work rancorous,
ingesting pain to pay for flight.

Some mornings I'm the milkweed,
rooted where I did not choose,
weathered by the sun
and violating winds.
Some mornings I'm the larva,
taking in the rugged leaf,
trusting, without knowing,
that swallowing transforms.

We think joy must be sweet,
but monarchs know.
They eat what they receive.
They hang where they have found.
They grow where they are dark.
But when they rise into the August air,

there is no taste of leaf, just open sky,

and through a season's calm,

unspoken prayer,

they see the milkweed far below,

splitting rough-hewn husks,

and casting seeds

into the sunset's russet glow.

Schadenfreude

Thank God he's dead.
I interject
to say again, he's dead;
thank God for that.
Samaritan illusion

came and went, pilfered
by a libertine
anathema: the man
who tripped upon
a rock once thrown

by his own hands,
drowning in his
own bath drawn,
inspired dose
of liquid vengeance.

I would have drawn it
for him, if he hadn't.

Shakespeare on Dating

Suicide, thy name is Woman.
Men have bled into eternity for love,
and am I to be made of stone,
touched by none?
But I have put the knife to work again.

A woman's love bleeds all.

Sisyphus

Tribulations endure
Until the gods see us remade
Or see that our remaking is in vain.
What then, when all is lost,

Eternally regretful
At hard-heartedness? Mindless pain
Remains my path, up this crag-mired terrain,
Where when the boulder falls

I pay for all my vices,
Brought from kingship to eternity
In Tartarus, a sweated penalty
Of labor. So be sure

Offenses always come,
But cursed are those by whom they come.
And those who scorn at their mortality,
those who store up vanities,

Prepare yourself for penance.
All your life a joy has hovered
Just beyond the grasp of consciousness.
The day will surely come

When you awake to find

Beyond all hope that it's attained

Or, like me, that it was yours to gain,

And you've lost it, perfectly.

An African Moon through Palms

An alabaster stepping stone
rises from a Roman sea towards Africa.
She flirts with me, like Isis poised, alone
behind the feathers of a palm,
beckons me to fall before her goddess-glory,
obscuring stars and making black sky blue
around her crown. When the wind moves
I see her porcelain face, lightsome in the breeze.
She poses nude and framed in effete light,
a scene, I'm sure, replayed again
a coquette, catching now a lost man's lonely gaze
over the sea, into the southern night.

Dear Seamus Heaney,

All month the quiet yearning in my soul
Has been to know what makes your writing so
Endearing, so uniquely filled with spirit?
Now I dream of pen-and-papered eloquence,
Gifted by your muse, who, after traveling
'Cross Ahab's sea, might come to visit me.
Of that good spirit I would ask to give
The life you've sown into your paper fields,
And all the fruit it yields to make a feast.
But what makes you so different, since I,
A man like you, can write and show emotion too?
Maybe it's the land you dwell where elves
Are poets singing ballads Tolkienesque.
There, mystic safety lies, and all facade
Is driven off like snakes in Patrick's wake
Of God. So many questions, so little time;
Funny how the same holds true for rhyme.

But you have found the time until
You die. What then, Masterful Poet,
Of shining Nobel Prize? May it recite
To souls after the grave, exhorting on
In inked visions left behind and realized.
Have you achieved success and meaning too?

I was to call this *Birth of a Poet*

To honor your placental works of art,

But I thought otherwise.

For on birthdays it is best to reminisce

How one arrived at his condition.

And so have I. I've thought you through and seen

This vision: I am me, and you are you,

The great divide between us and the men

We have become is like that unversed scope

Across our amaranthine sea,

       Though I hope one day you'll write.

       Fondly yours, Me.

Divine Voyeur

But that is what I hear, told she's coming,
and God is in it too. I hope it's true,
that lust lived out in white will then be mine.
But on that hallowed night let's not bring up
the fact that He'll be there.

We are galvanized, actuated heat,
impassioned sweat and fragrant moist release
of guimpe and alb, indulgent fever pitch
and soul egalitarianism.
It's odd to contemplate

He's in this moment, though we shouldn't mind.
I mind. To think, I call Him father,
not a sex-crazed and nymph-like deity
more fitting found in paganistic rite.
My father hoists me up

in muscled arms. I wait with bated breath,
as through a sea of stars and dappled blue
He moves me, away from perverse frictions,
toward a different kind of life, a night
where she, who is faceless,

lies nude and shadowed by his pearl-light moon.

My desire suits this. He sets me down

beside His flesh-robed soul reflection,

a generous perfection, poised, like me

in bed, and makes us whole.

Haymarket

Keep moving! Come the calls
in drawls distinct as Boston.
The people move like bees
inexorably towards pollen,
like water, swirling around
itself, gushing, rippling,
then stopping up at the dam
of a good deal on ripe fruit.

Kaleidoscopic colors
sold, purchased, and replaced
as if in tireless supply.
The smell emasculates the air,
now sweet and sticky, but with a tinge
of rot, though not enough
to objurgate the senses,
tipping on the edge of fusty.

They are the fruit of the earth
in carts, boxes, sneakers,
displaying souls on faces,
like their vegetative
counterparts. They fill the air
with odors, hues, and sound-life,

a baroque metonymy
of spirit on display.

Beside me, on the bench
before the vendor's cry and ware,
are two small boys, fish who swim
cross-current, confiscate
their father's peace, their colored
faces lit by sun and wonder.
Wide-eyed and toothy-grinned,
they wave and disappear again

among the moving wood of legs
with hanging fruit that swings
kinetic, back and forth, in wind,
and then they re-emerge.
They grip each other's hands,
and an apple. I wonder
whether there are too many here,
and if no one picks them
will they all, then, go to waste?

I Discussed Politics with the Gods
Last Night

I discussed politics with the gods
last night, on Mt. Olympus, illumined
by a deep-hued, glossy blue, with their facades
rimmed round a table of obsidian,
a debilitating white, aglow
like oil lamps auraed in a heavy night.
Zeus, his coal eyes terrifying what is seen,
postured by the goddess consort at his right,
aged Hera, glorious as the hero
Deborah, Hellenic warrior and queen,
fearful in her simple depth of wisdom.
On mighty Zeus' left, a sight of glory:
Athena, beautiful and awesome
in her terror. War was in her eyes to see
the blood of martyrs blemishing her candid
crimson crease of blood-stained lips held tight in thought.

Among the others that I well remember,
Cupid sat in handsome frame befitted
for a god: desire fleshed in ardor,
but for his wings, its feathers wrought
from gold to dazzle eyes, his only cover
aiding him to fly, a plague of arrowheads

determined to entrap and slay a lover.
Yet tired, bored, or filled with shame, his head,
within his arms, was laid upon the table.
The gods had turned their disapproving stares
on his rebellion once or twice before,
and Aphrodite, goddess of immobile
love was gone. I was let in on this affair,
the same committee that had played provocateur
to the fates of Troy, Crete, Sparta, Athens
and Atlantis. Now they plan this country's fate.

America stands poised upon Poseidon's
triton point, before it falls away, too late
to find escape from the self-created murk
and muddle of its tangled web of dreams.
Even self-indulgent, petty gods as these
look down from on their mountained handiwork
revolted to contempt at our extremes,
our loveless, hedonistic blasphemies.

Perhaps these calculating deities
commission me to constitute a message,
their voice, the word, and me a trinity
of evil omens on a pilgrimage
to devastate the earth and bring its end.
The epistle signaling the coup de grace,

a promise of apocalyptic doom,

is surely written in semata lugra,

for one of them, the sinner's friend,

and with it all I, too, will be consumed.

Iceberg

I reek of breaking,

float alone in Arctic fathoms,

a danger to all

who see the tip,

my visible being

the self

who sails upon its antipode.

Circumnavigate

my borders, but stave your way

or risk the gauntlet

of my presence:

shepherding the loss

of souls

to a Protean persona.

But the sun melts

at times. It warms above the waves,

and then I roll,

the weight of me,

the stark threat of edge

exposed

until I've gone to water,

able to lift men up,

not drag them down.

In The Beginning

It is my creation.

I formed it with my word.

My Son of God,

my incarnation

formed by my own hands.

It is a part of me,

and if it stands rejected

what is left but grief,

eternally?

It is who I am.

My nature, reflected.

Into the Wardrobe

I

You were standing there.
The party over,
silence filled your house,
in a peopled place
now filled with empty plates
and hollow glasses,
humming conversations'
echo ringing in your ears.
You were standing there.
At the threshold,
after stumbling
down the steps I turned
and saw you smiling,
reminding me
you've made a lasting
love and memory,
and you'll be on your way.
I wondered when
this wanderlust
came knocking at your door,
settled in your hearts
to beckon you
into the wardrobe,

out onto an open
everlasting road.

II

It stands before you now. Heavy wooden doors,
dark with mystery, carved in fine designs
of choices made and chiseled memory,
summon you to open them and journey through.
You can smell the air. It shouldn't be there,
foreign to a closet where for years
you've hung your heavy coats. It smells of change.
It smells of coast and waves, of pallid moonlight,
early morning rain, aromatic meadows
crowned with rocks thrust miles to the heavens,
with all the other wonders you will find.

You take a step, push through your lifeless
old and moldy clothes, and there it is:
a light that blinds, soaks you in a brighter sun,
'till you adjust to see the land spread out
to misted valleys, where the air is fresh,
spellbound, and discovery is breath.
You'll be spirited away until pursuit
succumbs to destiny in that faire state,
cared for by a great majestic king,

where the wind blows at his mane's shake,
and, at his roar, the earth quakes.

He's on the move.

III

As a thousand years is like a day,
those months will seem to you when you have reigned

upon that castled hill of liberty.
Look down on all you've done to see the way,

a journey home grown thick and overgrown
to stumble back through tear-stained wooden doors,

and all the fast-forgotten memories
won, regained to coalesce once more,

but only after struggling through coats
and scents you've left behind, you'll turn and seal

the doors. But though you will have traveled
there and back again, remember where you've been,

for like that never-ending sky, the road

you travel here at home will never end.

Leaving Armageddon

When I'm older, I will say
that I was handsome once,
when you didn't love me.

I saw you in a hundred faces,
pursued you, through dry and arid places,
where moth and rust and vultures
picked my bones
till I was withered dry.

So rise with Spirit-breath
in Armageddon, rise
with sinew, flesh and life
by the calling of the man of God,
and we will leave this place

together.

Nephilim

I have left the palm and date trees
to overtake the Nephilim,
lords indomitable, who watch
expectant for the sons of God,
their fathers.

The Preux Indians, with bronzed skin
and verdant feathered headdresses
cascading down their backs: for me
they wait, they overrun, they stand
triumphant.

Phoebe and the Naiad

Two moons float
upon a mirror
filled with gloaming stars,
scintillate
to set the course
of another night.

One, a naiad
lonely on the mere,
like the mariner
and Coleridge
she contemplates
alone,

half-hearted
dips her head
in search of Phoebe,
where she saw
her gazing back.
She keeps looking

pertinently hapless,
drowning in
an eidolon

of mist, a Carmelite

in de profundis

silence.

Poor Icarus

I

Stave off the waves, I yell, but it's no use.
He has fallen to the Lorelei,
whose sweet enticements followed him
into the sky, fly higher still,
until the sun deflowered both his wings,
picked them one by one.

                        Then an abstract
rush of wax, feather, flesh and human fowl
tumbled. By the Acherontic Sea,
helpless to assist I am a shadow
of the boy, a passing billow of a man
who stood upon the fold. Poor Icarus.

II

Poor Icarus. His eyes are discs
of bloat. Peculiarities
a little more amphibious,

but not nearly enough. He roils

in his memories of breath
and wishes for another one to take

as oxygen and life begin
to fade, like ink upon the palimpsest,
and all his thoughts are gone but one:

It would be nice to write this down.

Question

When I'm old,

will my eyes turn

brown seals

that disappear

beneath the insight

of the surface,

into oil depths,

where all that exists

is memory

and feeble breath?

Sieur De Monts

Cool beneath Acadian granite mounds,
I'm prodded gently by the breeze
in the wildflower gardens
of the Sieur de Monts.
The air is delicate, infused jouisance,
secreted with the flowers' scent,
disparate to the naked thrashing
of the ocean swells
on cliffs and gangling rocks that leave
the awed and trembling observer
sailing towards horizon,
more aware, more afraid
of my life-blood's meanness
thrashing naked through my veins.

So instead I ramble to the servile lull
of wood and stream.
The flowers offer up their honeysuckle smell
with woad and madder
blueberries, replete with juice,
for nose and eyes,
a dry and greedy mouth.
And for my ears the birds,
whose songs cascade

on branches, intertwine
with the rustling of leaves.

I'm a god of the Hesperides,
a modern day Edenic first-man
blanketed by solitude, the center,
having found significance,
or the appearance thereof, again.

The Prayer

She is inviolate and poised
upon the precipice.
The rock rises up, catches her
and she, though still, journeys,
set like the masthead of a ship,
withstanding the maelstrom.

Her hair entangles with the wind
like a thousand flags of peace
beneath the nettled firmament.
Dressed in black, enveloped
in the yare wings of a blackbird
flapping, pulling, pushing

up, up, up, and higher still
ever nearer Heaven.
Her hands are clasped below her waist
simply, at rest, closed
like her eyes. She is seeing God,
hearing His call: fly! Fly!

The elements swirl around her,
drawing up her prayers,
a murmur grown into a Voice
to the One who hears.

And her words, pledged, petitioned,

chase the wind, availing much.

Seventh Circle

Slowly, molassing round its border
Like hardening cement, runs crippled time.
I am a captured, tortured prisoner
Of boredom's reign, made wholly mine.

Her fumbling, whining cacophony
De-humanizes, martyrizes all.
Long after school bells ring to let us free,
It racks us with her monotoning call.

Amidst the thoughts that all my trouble's done,
Of bounding in escape from my duress
Through endless fields, below a golden sun
That burns away the agonizing stress,

The clock still ticks. My apostatic fate
Is realized again, for here I fell,
Down from my blessed catatonic state,
Into the wood of Dante's seventh hell.

The Trojan War in Myth and History

Struggles between right and wrong decisions,
the same old song worn out, the same old, same old
fighting to be different, then
to listen when I'm told,

"Obey! Do right or pay the price,"
while constipated conscience wallows good
in stagnant, fetid misery
thanks to a heavy cost,

like rotting here, perpetual madness
growing in my mind,
like sitting here, in sadness.

Did you know, Oh fascinating Helen,
students millennia removed would weep
not for the ships, a thousand sent,
but for the classes taught

about your sensual escapade.
Perhaps the horrors, washed over Ilion
for sins that you committed there,
would be welcome when compared

to being baptized in the torture faced

by those who follow

in a hollow, scholared waste.

The Way It Is

My lids are heavy still, but useful,
peering through my lack of sleep at sandy-hair
and sandy eyes; we're both well-worn.
The light, a growing saffron glow,
reflects your earnest face, a mouth that chews your thoughts
and spits them out in prayer and ennui:
as it should be.
Friends as brothers, reminiscing;
times like this come few and far between.
The clock and breath and life go on,
as do our many words released into the troposphere,
soaked up, received by God.

Tennis-matched ideas

                    are tossed between us.

Good intentions, volleyed aspirations
fly contained within each played-out ball,
and in this match our hearts and skills become refined,
born of different blood yet blood-born kin the same in time.

Wait.

Can it be? The match complete already?

128

Borrowed time is burning steady still,
and yet, I better go,

although, I wish you'd stay,
a rook among the pawns
upon the chessboard
of the White King watching,
for another game, another day.

But what will be your strategy?
Where, now, will you move?

Getting up, the lawn chair creaks beneath me;
trees rustle, birds sing, but silence closes in.
Near the gate I turn to you and say unsure,
See you next week and nothing more.
Words cannot express what friendship understands.

I close the gate and sigh, tired but at peace.

The Widow's Prophet

I

Heaney, give to me
a double portion
of your spirit.
I can see you
rising up to heaven
in a chariot
built by the prophets
of our trade. Promise then
to leave your mantle,
empower me
to cross the Jordan dry.

II

I watch her
fixing bread.
Itinerant
hands kneed
furiously,

interrupted
only when they sweep

against her floured
pinafore.
Reticent

in keeping back
an expletive
of hunger
and frustration,
she has barely

any left,
only morsels
maybe less,
and she strains
to feed me too.

III

Day and night she labored
having harrowed in hard scrabble.
Like morning mist her mettle and her gain
dissipate as quickly as her husbands.
Her home was desolate and raw as ice,
except the bills that spired on her kitchen
counter top, a modern-day Babel.

In the midst of this the prophet passed
outside her window, and held a pen
and notebook like a scribe.
"Have mercy," she cried,
but seeing her dejected state,
the man replied, "What can I do?"

Then an epiphanic vision
showed the future's unwrapped
possibility. So he had her gather
all the oil flowing in her blood,
multiplying it like loaves by Galilee
until the books were full,
with not a passage more.

The prophet gave it all to her,
instructed, "Go and sell it. Pay your debts,
then you may live on what is left."
And he moved on, beyond the bourn
of her existence, which remained forever
steeped in salient serenity at last.

IV

Spilled out to anoint the sick,
a Jubilee for masses stationed,

waiting to receive what I can give.
Since the oil given to the prophet
did not cause the woman any less,

use me like the widow's manna.
Pour me, though I may exhaust one day
when I can tip no more, and tears that will
not spill forever bless me
with the ewer filling to the brim again.

V. Shadows & Fire

Therefore I Am

I think,

I eat, sometimes too much and with regret,
cannot enjoy what's entering my mouth
when the pieces chewed
flood eyes when body comes to mind,
and I'm ashamed.

I work, no sweat, but toil nonetheless,
drowning slowly in a dead-end sudor
of monotony,
a sea of existential dread
and urge to surface.

I sleep, restless trying once for all
to satiate my body's pleasure-cry,
a cavernous desire,
exhausting 'till I stumble home, shamed,
to dream again.

I pray, on blood-stained knees before the love,
an unrelenting mercy that undoes,
crying, begging, shouting,
a child's push against a mountain.

In fact, it moves.

I laugh, seeing why it's worth the wait
to eat, to work, to sleep, to dream, to pray.
I am protagonist,
apple in an author's eye, to know this,
and then to laugh.

I write.

Through the Ash

From within the heart
actions betray purpose to the sun,
like seeds that go

     twisting,

         curling,

             pressing

through earth-time,
more ash than soil.

Perseverance and aplomb
allows for the heavens'
penetration.

It waits for what lay
hopeful in its cracking corn-crust,
which bursts for you
and, kissing dew,
intertwines my darkness
with your revealed light.

Time

It hits me like a six-ton brick:
regret upon a naked back,
regret for who I am,
and who I am is one
of time's uncertain outcomes.

It moves ahead of me,
motions me to dance
over a cliff,
where the bottom lies
six inches or six miles
from the edge.

When I Grow Up

Bullies chased me round the schoolyard
and once my mother saw me cry,
so I clenched my teeth and tearfully vowed,
'When I grow up.'

At times, Dad forced me into bed.
I'd thrash and kick, swimming through the air,
and then I'd yell with grand bravado,
'When I grow up.'

When my eyes hurt from the homework,
or when kids would laugh when I was picked
last for sports, then feebly I'd cry,
When I grow up.'

And I grew up.

One day I realized that I grew up,
that I walked my years like well-worn miles
and turned out poles apart from where I'd been.

So I felt like going back, returning
to my mother's arms, to those rebellious,
thrashing legs, stilled to sleep beside my old man.

And I did return.

I found it gone or different
or unreservedly the same.
They said that everyone had moved
or died, and so I left again.

Then I battled for my bread,
for my house, my job, my rights:
to be seen and heard once more,
to share my own opinion,
to fall in love and find the one
with whom I labored underneath
the borrowed heaviness of time,
and then we multiplied and filled
the earth with all our children,
who never made it old enough
to say, 'When I grow up.'

How long ago those days, that road,
that man who fathered me,
that love who suckled me,
and still I hear the young ones say,
'When I grow up.'

Was I mistaken to be young?

But I was, on the day I wished,
'When I grow up.'

A Dryad In Winter

It seems like only yesterday I saw
a dryad dancing in the bloom of Spring,
and captured it, became its lover
when I took you by the arm and led you
out among the amaranthine flowers.

I was happy to have lived for years
within you, years that ever-came in waves
crashing over Summer waves: warm, constant,
making me forget the season's turning
and your waning's inexorable approach.

You remained the defining fragrance
of an autumn leaf that, with earthen smell
and color-blast undoes the growing dread
of Winter, comforting beneath my shoes,
echoing the hush of the first Fall-frost.

And I was happy, drifting off to sleep,
perchance to dream of your crystalline face,
still beside me, glass upon the surface,
a quiet lake enveloped by the moonlight
of another wadmal Winter's night.

A Writer's Life

A writer's life is lonely,
like the letter *a*
at the beginning of this sentence,
useful, bending the mind towards
a coherent set of thoughts,
the linguistic piston catapult,
but it's utterly alone,

just an *a*,

meaningless
without its poetry.

Ode to My Pipe

Last night I had a conversation with my pipe.
I felt tired: tired, bored, and empty,
as if I never existed.

I lit it slowly, took a drag, and watched the smoke
curling in the air like soup, remembering
the many things forgotten,

and I told them to it while I smoked.

I told of all my longings,
recounted the desires
planted in your kisses,
lamented your forgetfulness
and all the tears I suffered
from the love that left me
desolate, forgotten,
told of how it's possible
that no one really loves me,
I mean really loves me,
I mean just me, loves *me*,
because I've been alone,
refusing to pay tribute
to the baseness of the world,

that maybe I'm finished,
maybe I'm defeated
by my own tragic life,
that I've suffered and cried,
that I've struggled to the end
and laughed, that it's what I've won
for being understanding,
only to live desperate
in an empty world.

Last night I had a conversation with my pipe,
and, having turned tobacco into ash,
I notice how, in this sad poem,

only he has cared for me, as an only friend,
and in the end, was incinerated,
emptied by my melancholy sighs.

Being a Man

There are days that I'm tired of being a man,
of living under brawny expectations,
emasculated, every failure cutting
like a knife, making me a eunuch to virility
but never master, always peering
past my chest to see what's missing, smaller
than I would've liked, down my stomach's birth-sign,
past the hairs that cover like a welcome mat
to intimacy, though no one's ever home,
and again I sigh and am tired.

I'm tired of being a man in musk-heat bars,
drowning in a sea of men who toss
testosterone waves, frothing at the mouth
and whipping up winds, upon which I can hear
their soul-cry like a distant sea-bird's call,
the need to be noticed and named, man.
And no matter how I flap my arms
I'm swept away, failing to rise and walk
upon its surface, giving myself over
to fatigue and then I drown again.

Even now I'm tired of being a man,
on a rainy day as this, when the cage

doesn't seem to open very wide
and the sight of falling water soaks me
with its loneliness, an empty puddle
in your absence. Then I see that tears fall,
not rain, because I'm dry and tired and absent,
gazing on the gray sheen of a lost day,
without your love to shape me in the mud
of dust and tears until I become—

Devices and Desires

Forgive, Almighty and most Merciful,
for I have sinned and strayed like wayward sheep.

With her I was mistaken, mistaken,
and this perfect trinity of disillusion
moved upon the surface of the deep.
Mistaken, though I met her in a church,
and watched her silently, unwilling to disturb
the prayers that, for me, were sacred.
The chalice of her lips; the halos
floating in her eyes, brown like the mud
placed by Christ upon the beggars lids
to sanctify his sight, though she was blind;
her face, reminiscent of the Panaghia.
Because of these and many other things,
I could have sworn . . .

But she was Ishtar, mother of the gods,
prima donna, venerated saint, then diva
teaching me her liturgy,
her capacity for solace,
reliquary to my loneliness,
and in the end she gave me nothing
but abandonment and heartache,

yet I saw her in a church,
that pall face covering a world of pretense
and I could have sworn . . .

But I found a sad reality instead,
driven by my heart's devices and desires
to rely upon this delicate deception.
Only God knows why He placed her where I tread,
a path that led to death or reformation.

Lord, have mercy, sinner that I am,
confessing all his faults and penitent.

With her I was mistaken.

Discussion with My Future Self

I see your wrinkles, wonder
how you put them there,
creased upon your skin,
dry like the badlands,
an unconquerable
arrangement of the years.
And then your hair, it billows
like a cloud over
Arctic waters, dyed blue,
perhaps the remnant
of a day's impulsiveness
gone wrong, a trace remaining
at your temples.

As you slosh around that meal
with indentured teeth,
make smacking noises
with those slugs for lips: wet,
crinkled, moving slowly over
an abandoned sandwich,
I wonder if you see
yourself alone, staring off
into the room. And, if not,
then what exactly do you see?

your many years? the choices
made that led you here,
to this restaurant, alone?

Do you see your children,
dead, abandoned, left you
on your own, and why?
What are you thinking
behind those steely, gray eyes,
children snuggled in between
their quilts of furrowed flesh?
I want to, no, I need to
know what to expect.
I hope you can make sense
of all those years, those debts
to God and life, that you're as full
as your belly is right now.

Do Poets Have Encores

He left the stage,

empty but for applause,

when she asked

if poets have encores,

and I wonder if,

like a medical

condition, they're tacked

upon an otherwise

healthy body,

or surgically removed

like a kidney stone, wart,

or a deviated septum.

Do they have encores,

as if they'll ever dwell

beyond the doors of encore.

It's what they do,

how they persist,

produce again, again

to live, and then again,

each fellowship

of words is fleeting,

a nightclub filled

with random meetings,

letters drowned out,

the space between

their bodies unified

by the throbbing sound

of encore,

       encore,

           encore.

But when there is no more,

there is a dead poet,

though a man, like this stage,

may remain, empty.

Inside Out

If I were turned within,
inside-out, like the fleshy
robes of a bud's inner flower,
I would have no color,
the hidden parts laid bare,
no mother-of-pearl
lining inner walls
but rather darkness skinned
upon my soul in rock and mud.

If I were turned within,
the light that shines
from my facade
would then withdraw
into itself and disappear
to light my inner places,
and I'd shine less,
but be a better man.

Soren Kierkegaard's Flower

What is your worldview?

What is the paradigm

of such an unassuming self,

that sits there, so content in time,

when all you see is blue?

The Brooch

The brooch of Chaucer's prioress
read Amor vincit omnia.
I think upon it, sitting now
upon God's brooch
and the inscription on the sea:
it conquers all.

The March Of Life

I'm in the March of life,
neither winter nor spring,
an amalgamation
of victory and strife,
birthed in the hush
of disappointment's
aftermath.
Rife with expectations
of daffodils and the warbling
blackbird calls
with the salmon-berry
burst upon their wings,
it's almost time to wake.

World, wake up.
Spread the leaves
to soak up sun,
Leaves, the invisible season's
hope and image,
but the wind still bites,
streams still smother
under skins of ice,
and though the sun is bright,
it never makes it

through to warm the bones.

My imagination,
though alive
and putting two and two
together, remains enslaved
to what my eyes behold:
winter, resolutely soaked
into my world,
the earth and sky.

Apocalypse

My body trembles, wracked with earthquake-sobs,
breaking bone and crust and sinew,
beating waves through every earthen member:
child lost, a love abandoned,
truth - the glorious Son of God revealed,
and the world groans.

Foundations reel,
earth's blood seethes,
fire and water,
ash and smoke,
a darkened sun,
a reddened moon,
tormented souls,
weeping, gnashing,
the ground contorts
and folds.

I call to the mountains and rocks
to fall on me; they don't.
I search for death and endless peace
to bury me; it won't.
Its anger pounds me still
and crushes innards into dust

until, I'm left un-filled.

The waters of the deep burst forth.

The tremor strikes again.

The tremor strikes again,

and again,

and again,

and again.

But then,

clouds part, illumination breaking through,

and He appears, that secret lover, who

adorns the bride with joy, like birth pang's past,

descending on the ruins of the old at last.

Benedict's Finger

His finger points,
a pistol shot,
the gun raised slight,
the bullet not yet
reaching to the heart.

Rigo!

How you fell,
a friend struck back,
a man undone.

Bang!

A domino of color:
turmoiled blue and white,
crashing, rising,
froth and flesh and water,
and the blood-red burst
upon the coats of those
who came to test a saint.

It was Rigo's blood
that splattered there,

after the prophet's voice
that pierced the air:

"Son."

And still the prophet sat,
stone-still among the saints,
a sanctuary at rest.

The Hunter and the Hearth

I

My wandering firebrand,
white-breasted Bast,
you slip away without a trace,
vanish in the dappled moonlit grass,
and still I think,
do you remember us at all?

You return replete with bones,
with death, with feathers,
moonlight stitched into your fur.
Yet there you lie, asleep a king,
as if you never left,
as if I never let you in.

You are sweet with us,
with sweetness borrowed.
I touch your head, your ears, your chin,
and still your heart beats elsewhere,
half for the hearth,
half for the mythic hunt.

And still I wait,
foolish that I am,
while you slip away again,
to Hel and Helheim,
back from whence you came,
a home among the stars.

II

Perhaps you sleep
in the hollow of stone,
the earth warm
against your ribs;
or stalk alone
along the hedge,
ember-eyes lit
with amber fire,
pawprints vanishing
before the moon.

Perhaps you flit
a shadow's flight
beneath the fence,
or spark a torch-light
flame through woods,
or wander wild

164

with pagan gods,
and hunt with Skadi
on the ancient paths
of bloodlust burning
in your soul?

And when you're home,
murderous, but sweet,
you do not share
where you have been.
I touch your head.
You feign your innocence.
I feign belief.

About the Author

Seraphim George's work bridges nature, faith, and the human experience. He has published poetry in multiple literary journals and wrote an award-winning novel. Seraphim continues to write poetry and novels while working in Communications for non-profit organizations. He spends his free time in church, on the water, and in the written word, not to mention raising his three children with his wife, Juliana, and his cat, Kimchi. *The Floating World* is his first full-length poetry collection.

To read his other work and find out more about the author, visit www.seraphimgeorge.com.